KU-786-714

CONTENTS

SPORT AT THE LIMITS

SEEKING ADVENTURE

Do you enjoy playing sport? Maybe you play for a team and relish working together with your teammates to challenge your opponents. Or perhaps your passion is swimming, running, or cycling and you always work hard to beat your personal best?

You might enjoy watching sport – following your local football team through thick or thin, or watching the biggest names in tennis thrash it out during gruelling matches? Maybe you are an athletics fan, and love to see the fastest humans on the planet battling to set new records?

Ultimate sport

Most of the sport in our lives happens in stadiums and arenas, following rules and schedules. However, some sportsmen and sportswomen don't want to compete in an arena. They push themselves to the ultimate extremes, determined to explore how far they can go with their sport. This exploration can take them to wild and dangerous parts of the world and demand that their bodies make the ultimate effort. These people are sporting adventurers.

On top of the world – sporting adventurers push themselves to the limits for the biggest thrills … and the best views.

Charlotte Guillain

Raintree is an imprint of Capstone Global Library Limited, a company incorporated in England and Wales having its registered office at 7 Pilgrim Street, London, EC4V 6LB – Registered company number: 6695582

www.raintreepublishers.co.uk
myorders@raintreepublishers.co.uk

Text © Capstone Global Library Limited 2014
First published in harback in 2014
Paperback edition published in 2015
The moral rights of the proprietor have been asserted.

Produced for Raintree by
White Thomson Publishing Ltd
www.wtpub.co.uk
+44 (0)843 2087 460

Edited by Judy Barratt
Designed by Ian Winton
Original illustrations © Capstone Global Library Ltd 2013
Illustrations by Stefan Chabluk
Picture research by Alice Harman and Judy Barratt
Originated by Capstone Global Library Ltd
Printed and bound in China by CTPS

ISBN 978 1 4062 7415 8 (hardback)
17 16 15 14 13
10 9 8 7 6 5 4 3 2 1

ISBN 978 1 4062 7420 2 (paperback)
18 17 16 15 14
10 9 8 7 6 5 4 3 2 1

Guillain, Charlotte
Defying Defeat: True Stories of Amazing Sporting Adventurers. (Ultimate Adventurers)
A full catalogue record for this book is available from the British Library.

Acknowledgements
We would like to thank the following for permission to reproduce photographs:
Alamy pp. 25 (© AF archive/*Touching the Void*; directed by Kevin MacDonald for New Line; 5 September 2003); Alistair Humphreys p. 9 (© Alistair Humphreys); Anne-Flore Marxer pp. 32, 34 (© Anne-Flore Marxer/Matthieu Georges); Caters News Agency p. 5 (© catersnews. com); Corbis pp. 7 (© Christophe Dupont Elise/Icon SMI), 27 (© Charlie Munsey), 28 (© Gordon Wiltsie/National Geographic), 35 (© David Spurdens/www.ExtremeSportsPhoto.com), 38–39 (© Rick D'Elia); Dreamstime pp. 12 (© Aleksandr Stikhin), 20–21 (© Andres Rodriguez); Getty Images pp. 8 (© Pierre Verdy/AFP), 14 (© Bobby Model/National Geographic), 19 (© Franck Fife/AFP), 21 (© Shaun Botterill), 23 (© Yves Boucau/AFP), 29 (© Jonathan Ferrey), 31 (© Getty Images), 33 (© Karl Weatherly); Photoshot p. 37 (© Imago); Rondi Davies pp. 10, 13 (© 8bridges.org/Greg Porteus); Shutterstock pp. 1 and 41 (© Christophe Michot), 4 (© Billetskly), 6 (© Dainis Derics), 15 (© Przemyslaw Skibinski), 22–23 (© Galyna Andrushko), 24 (© Steve Estvanik), 26 (© Topseller), 39 (© Beelde Photography), 40 (© Vitalii Nesterchuk); SuperStock p. 17 (© Eye Ubiquitous); Wikicommons p. 39 (© Kayvz)

Cover photograph of extreme climber David Lama scaling a rockface in Zillertal, Austria, reproduced with permission of Alamy Images (© Alamy Images).

Dean Dunbar

Dean Dunbar has not allowed disability to stop him becoming a sporting adventurer. Born in Scotland, Dean had become partially sighted by the age of nine. His sight continued to deteriorate and in his 20s he was registered blind. He took this as a signal to start challenging himself! Dean's adventures have included bungee jumping from a helicopter, taking part in a sea-kayaking race, and competing in a five-day challenge that included swimming, running, cycling, and kayaking!

Dean Dunbar makes a tandem skydive in 1998 to raise money for the school for the blind that he had attended as a child.

THE AHANSAL BROTHERS
KINGS OF THE SAHARA

Stretching across North Africa, the Sahara Desert is covered with sand dunes that are moved and shaped by the wind as it frequently whips up sandstorms. The Sahara is incredibly dry, with no natural shelter from the Sun. How do you fancy going for a run there?

The Marathon des Sables

One of the toughest running races on the planet takes place in the Sahara. Over six days, competitors race around 250 kilometres (155 miles) across the sand. This adds up to about five-and-a-half marathons, all of them run in gruelling conditions. Heat and sand rip runners' feet to shreds and competitors often suffer from heat exhaustion. After each shattering day, they have to sleep in tents pitched on the sand, hoping to get some rest before facing the challenge of the next day. Despite all this, two brothers have made the race look easy for many years.

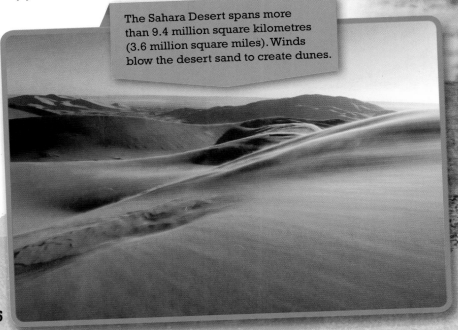

The Sahara Desert spans more than 9.4 million square kilometres (3.6 million square miles). Winds blow the desert sand to create dunes.

Lahcen and Mohamad

Lahcen and Mohamad Ahansal are from Morocco, where the Marathon des Sables is held. Lahcen, who works as a carpenter, has won the race an incredible 10 times. His younger brother, Mohamad, works as a mountain guide in the desert. He has won the race four times, setting a world record in 1998 as the fastest runner to cross the Sahara.

TOOLS OF THE TRADE

Forget about support teams! Marathon des Sables runners have to carry all the equipment they need on their backs. This includes sleeping bags and medical supplies, as well as food for the six days. Luckily, water is given to them at checkpoints.

Lahcen Ahansal (left) runs across the desert alongside his brother Mohamad (centre) and competitor Aziz El Akad (right) in the 2007 Marathon des Sables.

Becoming champions

Lahcen and Mohamad grew up in a poor family. When they first began to run in desert races, they had had very little training. But the boys were tough. As young children they ran to and from school across the desert every day, sometimes covering as many as 28 kilometres (18 miles). They became used to the difficult terrain of the Sahara, and they developed the stamina and fitness they needed to compete in extreme conditions.

When Lahcen and Mohamad first competed in the Marathon des Sables, they did not have suitable running shoes or proper equipment. Only as a result of competing and getting noticed did the brothers attract sponsors, who donated money so that they could equip themselves with such items as a compass, a pocket knife, and a signalling mirror.

The jubilant Ahansal brothers cross the finish line hand in hand, with Lahcen in first place and Mohamad in second place, in the 2005 Marathon des Sables.

Meryem Khali

Moroccan Meryem Khali came second of all the women who competed in the 2012 Marathon des Sables, running the race in 27 hours and 35 minutes. Meryem also competes in the tough steeplechase (an obstacle race) in international athletics competitions.

Ultra competitor

Mohamad found the 2006 race to be the toughest. A sandstorm blew up in the middle of the race, making conditions uncomfortable and disorientating for competitors. Mohamad runs with a pacer during the first and last stages of the race to help him keep up a fast pace. He eats a mixture of dates, honey, and nuts during the race to give him energy.

Alastair Humphreys

British adventurer Alastair Humphreys managed to finish the 2008 Marathon des Sables despite breaking his foot in the process! He has also cycled around the world, rowed across the Atlantic Ocean, and trekked across India, among other sporting adventures.

In 2012, Alastair Humphreys (back) and Leon McCarron (front) made a 1,600-kilometre (1,000-mile) trek across the Arabian Desert.

GRACE VAN DER BYL

MARATHON SWIMMER

What could be more enjoyable than a relaxing swim in a warm pool? But how would you feel about swimming 193 kilometres (120 miles) down a river, ending up in the harbour of one of the world's busiest cities? This was the challenge marathon swimmer Grace van der Byl set herself when she took on the 8 Bridges Hudson River Swim – the longest competitive open water swim in the world.

Grace's challenge

Born in the United States, Grace learned to swim when she was just two years old. By the time she was a teenager, she had become a competitive swimmer, representing her university in national swimming competitions. After this, she spent several years coaching other swimmers before getting interested in open water races – swimming competitions that take place outdoors, in oceans, rivers, lakes, and other bodies of water. Open water swimmers often have to deal with freezing temperatures, dangerously strong currents, and even jellyfish and sharks!

Grace van der Byl and Rondi Davies congratulate each other on completing another stage of the 8 Bridges Hudson River Swim, in 2012. Sun block protects Grace's face from the Sun's reflection on the water.

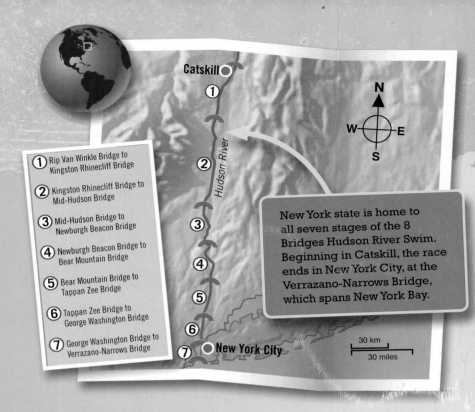

Catskill

① Rip Van Winkle Bridge to Kingston Rhinecliff Bridge

② Kingston Rhinecliff Bridge to Mid-Hudson Bridge

③ Mid-Hudson Bridge to Newburgh Beacon Bridge

④ Newburgh Beacon Bridge to Bear Mountain Bridge

⑤ Bear Mountain Bridge to Tappan Zee Bridge

⑥ Tappan Zee Bridge to George Washington Bridge

⑦ George Washington Bridge to Verrazano-Narrows Bridge

Hudson River

New York City

N
W · E
S

New York state is home to all seven stages of the 8 Bridges Hudson River Swim. Beginning in Catskill, the race ends in New York City, at the Verrazano-Narrows Bridge, which spans New York Bay.

30 km
30 miles

Other swims

Before attempting the 8 Bridges Hudson River Swim, Grace took part in several other open water races, including the Alcatraz Challenge Swim in 2010. This race takes place in San Francisco Bay, where the rough ocean water is only around 13 degrees Celsius (55 degrees Fahrenheit). During the race, Grace didn't even wear a wetsuit! She was the first woman to finish the race and second overall, beating all but one of the male competitors.

Team Grace

Grace's coach, Joe Benjamin, has worked with her since 2008. He accompanies her in a boat or on a paddleboard during competitions. Joe says that Grace is an easy person to coach: "She has a huge heart, both in and out of the water. So when you're training her that big heart makes it easy, because she'll do whatever you ask and give a thousand per cent."

Never completed before

There are seven stages in the 8 Bridges Hudson River Swim, and most swimmers undertake only a few of them. Grace, however, wanted to be one of the first people to complete all seven stages. Only two other swimmers had tried to swim the whole race before, in 2011, and both had failed. Before the 2012 race Grace said, "I am just going to take it one stroke at a time till I can't go anymore."

Martin Strel

In 2007, marathon swimmer Martin Strel, from Slovenia, achieved the world record for the longest swim, down the length of the Amazon River – all 5,268 kilometres (3,273 miles) of it! He has also swum the lengths of the Mississippi, the Danube, and the Yangtze rivers!

Route to victory

The 8 Bridges Hudson River Swim begins in the Catskill Mountains, with quiet countryside on either side of the river. Grace felt nervous before she got into the water, but relaxed once she started swimming. After the race, she wrote about the various stages, saying that Stage 4, between Newburgh Beacon Bridge and Bear Mountain Bridge, with its beautiful scenery, was one of her favourites. She described Stage 5 as "a beast" as the current was strong and the river became much wider, and busier with boats. When finally she reached the end of the race in New York Harbor, Grace had not only come first, she had also set a new record in every stage of the swim. Best of all, she had achieved her goal to complete all seven stages. The only other swimmer to do this was Rondi Davies from Australia, who was just behind Grace throughout the race.

Bear Mountain Bridge marks the end of Stage 4 of the 8 Bridges Hudson River Swim and the beginning of Stage 5.

TOOLS OF THE TRADE

Before the race, Grace had to eat plenty of carbohydrates to give her energy. The water in the river is very cold, so in order to keep her energy levels up and prevent hypothermia, Grace had to keep eating during her swim. She fed on a special carbohydrate drink, taking one every 20 minutes when she reached very cold sections of water.

The swimmers' coaches paddle alongside during the race to offer support. Swimmers pass some iconic sights on their way to the finish line, including the Statue of Liberty.

KIRA SALAK

PROFESSIONAL ADVENTURER

Kira Salak, from the United States, seems to be addicted to adventure. She has travelled all over the world on her own, reaching places that very few people have visited. Even though many of her travels take her through countries that others may think of as dangerous, Kira does not worry. In fact, she relishes the challenge and loves to meet people whom she would never discover on safer adventures.

Other feats

Kira has earned a Wisconsin state record for the fastest run over 1.6 kilometres (1 mile). She also practises tae kwon do and kickboxing, and mountain climbing without any equipment!

Early exploring

When Kira was in her 20s, she travelled around Africa with nothing but a backpack. This gave her a great sense of freedom and confidence, but also a taste of how dangerous exploring can be. While she was backpacking around Mozambique, where a war was being fought, soldiers kidnapped her. She escaped, but the experience taught her about the realities of danger. Her trip to Africa inspired her to backpack across Papua New Guinea – she became the first woman to cross the country.

Among her many adventures, Kira Salak crossed the Zagros Mountains, in Iran, on the back of a donkey in 2006.

Then and now

Kira has followed in the footsteps of many famous Western explorers. In the 19th century, Dr David Livingstone was the first European to see Victoria Falls, Lake Malawi, and many more of Africa's geographical features. He travelled on foot, with very little equipment, and relied on local guides to help him find his way and to carry his belongings.

The magnificent Victoria Falls were among the discoveries of British explorer Dr David Livingstone (1813–1873) as he undertook his adventures in Africa.

More adventures

Today, Kira travels all over the world, writing articles and books about her experiences. Many of her adventures have taken place in a kayak. She has kayaked 965 kilometres (600 miles) on her own along the River Niger to Timbuktu in Mali, West Africa, during the relentless downpour of the rainy season. She has also kayaked along the Irrawaddy River, in the Burmese jungle, in unbearably high temperatures. She spotted incredibly rare Irrawaddy river dolphins on the way.

On dry land, Kira has faced the challenge of climbing the Kaf Ajnoun mountain, a rock formation in the Sahara Desert in Libya, North Africa. Its name means Mountain of Ghosts and many local people believe it is haunted by genies. She is happy to explore on two wheels, too, and has cycled 1,287 kilometres (800 miles) across Alaska, from Anchorage to the Arctic Ocean.

> "Once the journey starts, there's no turning back. The journey binds you, it kidnaps and drugs you with images of its end, reached at long last. You picture yourself arriving on that fabled shore. You see everything you promised yourself."
>
> **Kira Salak**

1 Kira escaped from kidnappers in Mozambique

2 Kira was the first woman to cross Papua New Guinea

3 Kira kayaked 965 kilometres (600 miles) to Timbuktu in Mali

4 Kira kayaked through a jungle in Burma

5 Kira climbed the Kaf Ajnoun mountain in Libya

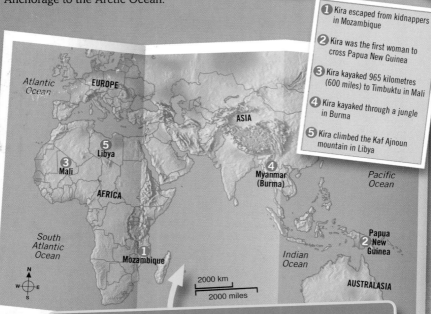

Kira Salak's expeditions have taken her all over the world. This map shows the locations of her major adventures.

Christina Dodwell

The British writer Christina Dodwell is another great explorer. She was stranded in Africa after her jeep was stolen during a holiday – and she decided to stay for three years! She travelled across the continent in a canoe, as well as by horse, camel, and even elephant. She was soon ready for more adventure and has since travelled around Papua New Guinea, China, and Siberia, among other places. On one daring trip, she flew a microlight aircraft for 11,265 kilometres (7,000 miles) across West Africa.

Christina Dodwell in Cameroon with a group of local men and children, and the microlight aircraft that took her across West Africa.

RACE2RECOVERY
TEAM INSPIRATION

In 2011, a team of volunteers came together with one aim in mind. This group of determined individuals planned to take part in the gruelling Dakar Rally, one of sport's toughest motor-racing challenges. Most of the team was made up of injured servicemen, some of whom had missing limbs or spinal injuries, as well as ex-servicemen and rally-driving experts. The team called themselves Race2Recovery.

The Dakar Rally

The Dakar Rally is a 8,575-kilometre (5,328-mile) off-road car race that used to run from Paris, France, to Dakar, the capital of Senegal in West Africa. In 2009, the rally moved to South America. The challenging route now runs through Peru, Argentina, and Chile, taking the competitors across deserts and over mountains. Rally drivers encounter sand dunes, rocks, and other rough terrain.

The Dakar Rally begins in Lima, Peru, crosses the Andes into Argentina, then crosses back to end in Santiago, Chile. The precise route changes every year.

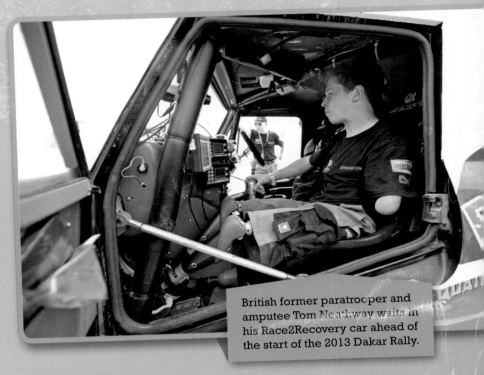

British former paratrooper and amputee Tom Neathway waits in his Race2Recovery car ahead of the start of the 2013 Dakar Rally.

Making history

Race2Recovery wanted to become the first disability team to complete the rally. Several members of the team had lost limbs in explosions in Afghanistan. One bomb blast had caused American Marine Sergeant Mark Zambon to lose both his legs, while another had resulted in British paratrooper Tom Neathway having to have both his legs and his left arm amputated. Also from the British Army, Andrew Taylor had been caught in an explosion that injured his back. These men, and all the other members of the team, shared a determination and spirit that would make sure they made it to the Dakar Rally in 2013.

Cathy Derousseaux

Cathy Derousseaux was the only woman in the Race2Recovery team, and she was also among its most experienced rally drivers. One of the team's able-bodied members, she had already won the French Women's Rally Championship twice and had worked on a support crew for the Dakar Rally in 2007.

Preparing for the race

The team spent months in training, as well as testing and adjusting their vehicles, before they were ready for the challenges of the Dakar Rally. This preparation included going to Morocco, where drivers could get used to driving over sand dunes and rocky tracks in the Atlas Mountains. Amputee drivers also had to adjust to the problem of sand, dust, and high temperatures interfering with the smooth working of their artificial arms and legs.

The 2013 Dakar Rally

The Race2Recovery team sent four cars to the rally in January 2013, each with a driver and co-driver, as well as a number of support vehicles. Only one of the rally cars made it through to the end of the race, but this car represented the whole team to claim success for Race2Recovery – the first team with disabled drivers to finish the Dakar Rally.

The drivers who finished, Major Matt O'Hare and Corporal Phillip Gillespie, had to drive over mountains and across desert, as well as through floods, to reach the finish line. Afterwards, Major O'Hare said, "To complete the Dakar Rally is an incredible achievement in itself, but to become the first ever disability team to cross that finish line lifts the achievement to a whole other level."

One car makes a dramatic skid as it races across the sand in the Peruvian leg of the 2013 Dakar Rally.

Team inspiration

The Race2Recovery team's motto is "Beyond injury – achieving the extraordinary". By taking part in races, the team raises money for a recovery centre where injured servicemen and servicewomen can spend time recuperating. Race2Recovery also inspires everyone who faces injury, disability, or other difficulty.

On Day 10 of the race, Major Matt O'Hare and Corporal Phillip Gillespie, the duo that completed the rally for the Race2Recovery team, make a splash in Córdoba, Argentina.

JOE SIMPSON
FEARLESS MOUNTAINEER

Imagine what it would be like to climb to the top of the world's highest mountains. You could be far from anyone other than your climbing companions. Freezing wind or rain, or even snowstorms, could whip around you. You would have to carry enough oxygen to be able to breathe – so what would happen if you ran out? You could be buried in an avalanche or fall to your death. Does it sound like a hobby *you'd* like to take up?

Born to climb

Joe Simpson is a British mountaineer who is renowned for his near-death experiences on mountains. As a teenager, he read a book that described some of the dangers involved in climbing, but for some reason he was not put off and instead he took up climbing as his hobby. During his early 20s, Joe climbed mountains around the world, managing in the course of his adventures to survive an avalanche, a fall, and hanging off a ledge for 12 hours waiting for help. But this was just the beginning.

Physical risk

Over the years, Joe's climbing injuries have included:
• broken ankles
• a neck injury
• a shattered knee
• a broken spine
• arthritis.
Sadly, he has also had many friends who have died while they were climbing.

An avalanche happens when snow tumbles down a mountainside, gathering speed as it travels, swallowing everything in its path.

David Lama

From a young age, David Lama showed a talent for climbing. In 2006, at only 15 years old, he was allowed to enter the Free Climbing World Cup. Free climbers take on sheer rock faces, using their hands, feet, and body (rather than equipment) to make the climb. The World Cup is made up of several competitions. David came second in the first competition and won the second, finishing second overall. Since then, he has gained fame for climbing some of the most difficult mountains in the world.

David Lama on a climbing wall during the 2006 International Mountaineering and Climbing Federation's Free Climbing World Cup in Belgium, when he was only 15 years old.

Andes ordeal

In 1985, Joe travelled to Peru with his friend Simon Yates to climb the Siula Grande mountain in the Peruvian Andes. The west face of the mountain had never been climbed before and the two climbers successfully reached the summit. However, as they were coming back down, bad weather caused Joe to slip and break his leg.

Siula Grande is 6,344 metres (20,814 feet) high, making it the second highest peak in the Cordillera Huayhuash region of the Andes.

The Andes mountain range covers around 8,900 kilometres (5,500 miles) down the length of South America. Siula Grande lies in Peru, in the northern Andes.

Venezuela
Colombia
Guyana
French Guiana
Suriname
Ecuador
Peru
Siula Grande
Brazil
Bolivia
Paraguay
Chile
Uruguay
Argentina

Pacific Ocean
Atlantic Ocean

THE ANDES

N
W E
S

1000 km
1000 miles

Lost and found

The climb had taken longer than Simon and Joe had planned, so their supplies were already low. They had run out of fuel for their stove, so they were unable to melt snow for drinking water. They needed to get down fast. Simon began to lower Joe on a rope, but the rope got caught and the weather and darkness meant that Simon could not free it. The two friends were now at different heights but attached to the same rope. Joe could not climb back up and Simon could not pull him back up. Both their lives were at risk. In the end Simon had to cut the rope so that he could get down safely. As Simon did so, Joe fell into a crevasse.

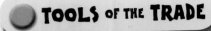
TOOLS OF THE TRADE

The most important tool for a mountaineer is rope. Even though Joe fell because Simon cut the rope that was holding him, that same rope helped save his life. He was able to get to safety only by tying the remains of the rope around his body and lowering himself down to a ledge that ultimately led out of the crevasse.

Somehow Joe survived the fall, landing on a ledge and digging out a hole for shelter. Then, he managed to lower himself further into the crevasse, before climbing onto a glacier. Despite having no food and very little water, Joe survived for another three days, managing with his broken leg to crawl back to safety. Simon, having assumed his friend must have died, could not believe his eyes when Joe arrived back at base camp.

Joe Simpson climbing in the Andes in 2003 during the filming of *Touching the Void*, the movie that recounts the story of his and Simon's ordeal.

STEVE FISHER
COOL KAYAKER

Have you ever spent time in a kayak or a canoe? Paddling along a river or across a lake can be a relaxing way to explore the great outdoors. Some people, however, like to take the experience to a completely different level.

Getting started

Steve Fisher grew up on his family's farm in South Africa. He got into his first kayak when he was only six years old and was soon taking part in kayak racing competitions. When he was 21, Steve began to kayak full time in the rapids on the Zambezi River. Steve was always looking for bigger and wilder challenges and so he started practising the most extreme form of his sport – freestyle kayaking.

Freestyle kayakers hone their paddling skills in order to perform amazing somersaults.

Freewheeler

Steve was soon an expert freestyle kayaker. In 1998, he performed a new move, the world's first Freewheel. To do this, he cartwheeled his kayak down a waterfall. He helped create moves called the Air-screw, the Helix, the Flip-turn, the Silly Flip, and the Pan-am. He also dedicated himself to improving kayak design for his sport. Eventually, though, having won many freestyle competitions around the world, Steve needed a new challenge. This time it would be exploration in a kayak.

Steve Fisher rides the wave sideways in his kayak, on a river near Egmont, British Columbia, Canada.

What is freestyle kayaking?

A competitive sport, freestyle kayaking involves playboating, during which the paddler has to perform a range of special moves in the kayak while descending whitewater rapids. The moves include spins, loops, flips, and turns, often combined into complicated sequences.

New adventures

Steve set his sights on exploring the world's wildest rivers, aiming to be the first to paddle down their dangerous rapids. His first expeditions included the Irrawaddy River in Burma and the Salween River in China. In 2002, he took a team to the TsangPo River in Tibet, kayaking down the whitewater rapids that flow through one of the world's deepest gorges. The TsangPo gorge is three times deeper than the Grand Canyon in the United States, measuring 6,009 metres (19,714 feet) at its deepest point. Nobody had ever successfully paddled along the Upper Gorge section. In fact, some explorers had died during their attempts.

Flowing over rocks and boulders, creating dangerous rapids, Tibet's TsangPo River curves around Mount Namcha Barwa, which is more than 7,780 metres (25,500 feet) high, in the Himalaya mountain range.

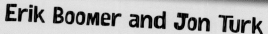

Erik Boomer and Jon Turk

Explorers Erik Boomer and Jon Turk were the first to paddle their kayaks around the remote Ellesmere Island in Canada. Their Arctic expedition covered 2,390 kilometres (1,485 miles) and took them 104 days. At times they had to drag their kayaks across ice. They also had to ski and hike, and they even came face to face with polar bears!

Over the edge

At one stage along the river, Steve and his team came across a steep drop. The team climbed out of the water to re-enter further along – but not Steve. He slid his kayak off a rock and paddled between boulders before shooting over a 3-metre (10-foot) waterfall. The team watched as Steve disappeared into the foam. When he resurfaced, Steve paddled hard to escape the currents that tried to pull him under. This had been a close call – one of many on the trip. The team had to end the expedition before reaching their planned finishing point, but they did succeed in being the first team to descend the Upper Gorge successfully.

Steve Fisher drops into the 9-metre (30-foot) Big Brother Falls, Washington state, United States, during the Extreme Kayaking Finals of the Ford Gorge Games in 2002.

From A to Z

Steve's kayaking adventures have taken him all around the world, from the River Amazon in Brazil in 2005, where he surfed on a tidal bore in his kayak, to Zambia in 2008, where he led a team down the Zambezi River rapids.

The ultimate challenge

In 2011, Steve was part of a team that, after six years of planning and preparation, attempted the ultimate kayaking challenge of paddling down the Inga Rapids on the Congo River. The expedition took Steve to one of the world's most remote rivers and included the world's largest rapids. He and the team successfully travelled down an 80-kilometre (50-mile) stretch of rapids, waterfalls, and whirlpools. When one whirlpool sucked Steve under water, he almost drowned, but with sheer strength and determination he resurfaced and made it through to the end.

"If people forget everything else about me as a kayaker, in 50 years they will remember that Steve Fisher did the Inga. There was a long road up until this moment. It is the umbrella, a culmination of everything else I have achieved."
Steve Fisher

The Congo River is 4,700 kilometres (2,920 miles) long, and it flows through some of the most remote parts of Africa.

James Cracknell

James Cracknell is an ex-Olympic rower who has undertaken a huge range of sporting challenges. His adventures include:
• rowing across the Atlantic Ocean
• running, cycling, and kayaking 600 kilometres (370 miles) across Tasmania
• trekking to the South Pole
• running the Marathon des Sables (see pages 6–9), finishing 12th.
Unfortunately, in 2010, James was injured when a truck hit him as he cycled across the United States. Now he campaigns for cycling safety and the environment.

James Cracknell (front) paddles through the waves in the kayaking heat of the 2006 Pure Tasmania Challenge, set in Hobart, Australia.

ANNE-FLORE MARXER

SUPER SNOWBOARDER

Snowboarding is a sport full of fun and skill. Over time, snowboarders have developed different moves and tricks, practising jumps, half-pipes, and rails, a bit like skateboarders. But the most extreme form of snowboarding has to be freeriding. Also known as backcountry and all-mountain snowboarding, freeriding uses all the toughest snowboarding moves, but over wild terrain. The queen of this unpredictable sport is Anne-Flore Marxer.

Starting out

Anne-Flore grew up in Switzerland in a family of racing skiers. She took to the slopes when she was just one year old. Eventually, she decided to go her own way and chose snowboarding over skiing. When she was a teenager, she would often sneak off with her snowboarding equipment after school to train and take part in snowboarding competitions. Once she had mastered freestyle techniques, Anne-Flore was ready for the tougher and more exhilarating challenge of freeriding. She entered her first competition out of curiosity – and won!

Anne-Flore always wears a helmet when she is freeriding to protect her head if she falls. Her goggles block out the glare of the Sun and its reflection on the snow so that she can see where she is going.

An extreme skier launches himself from the face of a mountain into the powdery snow below.

Davorin Karničar

Davorin Karničar, from Slovenia, has become famous for extreme skiing. This involves climbing very high mountains and then skiing down them. Davorin's extreme-skiing conquests include:
- Mount Everest, the highest mountain in the world
- Mount Kilimanjaro, the highest mountain in Africa
- Mount McKinley, the highest mountain in North America
- Vinson Massif, the highest mountain in Antarctica.

Dangerous sport

Freeriding snowboarders face many dangers. The off-piste terrain is unpredictable, meaning that boarders often encounter rocks and uneven ground that can make them lose control. Freeriders risk getting caught in avalanches, when snow slides down a mountainside, burying everything in its path. When she freerides, Anne-Flore takes a shovel and a backpack with an airbag in case she is buried in an avalanche. She wears a helmet and carries a transceiver, a device she can use to communicate with her back-up team if she gets into trouble.

Freeride filming

Like many other freeriders, Anne-Flore films her snowboarding. She pushes herself to the limit to demonstrate the best moves in the most spectacular terrain for the movies that promote her sport. Although observers film some of the footage, Anne-Flore records some of it herself, using a camera attached to her helmet or even holding a camera in front of herself. In Alaska, Anne-Flore was filmed in difficult weather conditions jumping over large crevasses. Luckily she enjoyed the challenge!

Anne-Flore Marxer makes a near-vertical descent down a snowy mountainside in Haines, Alaska.

"I love the mountains, the freedom, and the peace. I love the snow on the trees, the silence, and the Sun glittering on fresh powder, the snowmen, the landscape from above the world, and the snowball fights, the hot chocolates, and the long runs of powder, even the short ones through the forest, the après ski, and the cold snow in your face ... I just love it all ..."
Anne-Flore Marxer

World champion

In 2011, Anne-Flore competed in four tough competition stages to become World Freeride Champion. She is now acknowledged to be one of the most adventurous snowboarders in the world and has been named Best International Rider of the Year.

Freeriding takes place through mountain forests. Riders have to develop skill to be able to leap across levels in the unpredictable terrain.

TOOLS OF THE TRADE

As she can snowboard only during the winter, Anne-Flore surfs, cycles, practises yoga, and trains in the gym to make sure she stays fit throughout the summer months, and until she can freeride again.

JURE ROBIČ

EXTREME CYCLIST

Many people enjoy going for a bike ride. After all, it is a great way to exercise and relax. Some people take it further, cycling long distances or racing other cyclists or the clock. But what happens when cyclists take their sport to the extreme?

Slovenian superman

Born in Slovenia in 1965, Jure Robič became a soldier in the Slovenian army and was a member of his national cycling team before going on to win some of the world's toughest cycling races. Possibly the most notorious of these is the Race Across America, a 4,830-kilometre (3,000-mile) coast-to-coast race across the United States. The riders have no scheduled breaks during which they can stop, rest, and recover – they just keep going for as long as they are able. The winner generally manages on very little sleep.

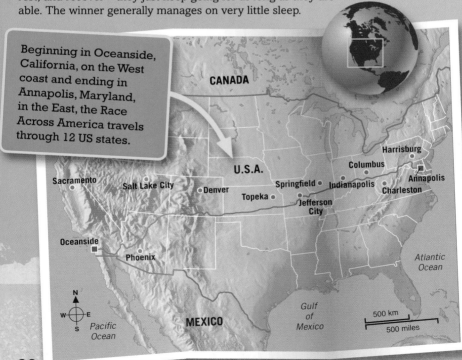

Beginning in Oceanside, California, on the West coast and ending in Annapolis, Maryland, in the East, the Race Across America travels through 12 US states.

CANADA

U.S.A.

Sacramento

Salt Lake City

Denver

Springfield • Indianapolis

Topeka • Jefferson City

Columbus

Harrisburg

Annapolis

Charleston

Oceanside

Phoenix

Atlantic Ocean

MEXICO

Gulf of Mexico

N W E S

Pacific Ocean

500 km

500 miles

Tim Skipper

Ultra-cyclist Tim Skipper, from the United States, has taken part in the Race Across America nine times, and has completed the race on tandems and recumbent bicycles. Altogether, he has achieved four course records! He has also won other marathon cycling races, including the Furnace Creek 508, an 817-kilometre (508-mile) race in California, and the HooDoo 500, an 837-kilometre (520-mile) race in Utah. He is good on his feet, too, and has run the Los Angeles marathon twice.

Record maker

Jure won the Race Across America five times, becoming well known for surviving the competition on barely any sleep at all. In 2004, he cycled approximately 560 kilometres (350 miles) a day for eight days, sleeping for only eight hours in total during the entire Race Across America. Perhaps unsurprisingly, this feat earned him a place in the record books.

Jure Robič shows grim determination and incredible stamina during a cycle race.

French challenge

In 2005, only six weeks after his second Race Across America victory, Jure won Le Tour Direct. Another gruelling race without scheduled breaks, Le Tour Direct takes place over a 4,025-kilometre (2,500-mile) course that is made up of the toughest cycling routes in France. Jure covered the distance, much of it up steep gradients, in an incredible seven days and 19 hours.

Tough training

Jure had to push himself extremely hard to prepare for and win these races. He trained for hours every day and often practised going without sleep for days at a time. He clocked up more than 45,000 kilometres (28,000 miles) on his bike every year, which is equivalent to travelling around Earth and a bit more! However, the excessive training and endless competing took their toll on Jure's body. His feet and hands would swell up towards the end of long races, and he often lost feeling in his thumbs as a result of gripping the handlebars for such a long time.

Extreme cyclists Marvin and Pamela Atwood cycle the highway through Arizona during the 2006 Race Across America. In 2005, the couple had been the first husband and wife and the first grandparents ever to compete in the race.

Then and now

Cycling has been blighted by competitors taking drugs to improve their performance. Lance Armstrong had been celebrated for winning the Tour de France seven times in a row, but now admits that he took banned substances in order to accomplish this feat. Today, many cyclists are campaigning hard to make sure their sport is fair and clean.

Lance Armstrong cycling in Colorado, United States, in 2012, the year before he went on television to admit to taking banned substances.

Cycling to the end

Very sadly, in 2010, Jure was cycling in the mountains of Slovenia when he collided with a car and died. He will be remembered as one of the toughest cyclists in history, who won more than 100 races during his career.

Jure Robič collecting his medal after winning the 2007 Race Across America, a race he won five times altogether.

WHERE NEXT?

PUSHING THE LIMITS

This book has looked at just some of the adventurers who have pushed themselves to the extremes of their sports. Many more take on new adventures and face new challenges every day. As technology enables us to continue to improve sports equipment, and sponsors enable elite sportspeople to take the time they need to train and compete, greater and tougher challenges will become possible.

A climber scales a vertical surface of ice formed by a frozen waterfall. This extreme sport is called waterfall ice climbing.

More extremes

Some other adventurers in the world of sport include Gary Hunt, a champion cliff diver from the United Kingdom, who dives from great heights, often amid spectacular scenery. Mike Libecki, from the United States, is an explorer, who climbs to some of the world's most remote places and then snowboards down or kite skis over frozen lakes. Ramon Navarro from Chile surfs on some of the world's biggest waves, risking his life in the process. Edurne Pasaban is a mountaineer who, in 2010, became the first woman to climb the world's 14 highest mountains. All these people share the qualities of determination, stamina, and self-belief that are needed to succeed at the limits.

Adventures in the future

As James Cracknell and Jure Robič show, sporting adventurers are willing to take risks and encounter danger that can lead to injury or even loss of life. Even though we might not know what new developments there will be in extreme sports in the future, we can be sure that sporting adventurers will always be making plans for the next expedition or challenge that takes them to the edge of possibility.

Leaping from a fixed base with a parachute strapped to your back is called BASE jumping. The BASE stands for Buildings, Antennae, Spans, and Earth (where "spans" means bridges and "earth" means cliffs) – the surfaces that make good launchpads for this extreme sport.

TIMELINE

1985 Joe Simpson (UK) survives falling into a crevasse while climbing down the Siula Grande in Peru.

1998 Mohamad Ahansal (Morocco) sets a world record as the fastest runner to cross a desert.

Steve Fisher (South Africa) invents the Freewheel move.

2002 Steve Fisher and a team of kayakers battle rapids along the TsangPo River in Tibet.

Kira Salak (USA) kayaks down the River Niger to Timbuktu.

2004 Jure Robič (Slovenia) sets the record for Race Across America, cycling 560 kilometres (350 miles) a day for eight days.

2005 Jure Robič wins Le Tour Direct.

2006 Steve Fisher kayaks along the River Amazon.

2008 Steve Fisher tackles rapids on the Zambezi River.

Mohamad Ahansal wins the Marathon des Sables for a second time.

2009 Mohamad Ahansal wins the Marathon des Sables for a third time.

2010 Grace van der Byl (USA) is the first woman to finish in the Alcatraz Challenge Swim.

Jure Robič is killed in a cycling accident.

James Cracknell (UK) finishes the Marathon des Sables in 12th place.

2011 Steve Fisher kayaks down the world's largest rapids on the Congo River.

Anne-Flore Marxer (Switzerland) becomes World Freeride Champion.

2012 Grace van der Byl wins the 8 Bridges Hudson River Swim.

2013 The Race2Recovery team completes the Dakar Rally, becoming the first disability team to do so.

Where would be the perfect place for you to run?
a At the local park, playing football with your friends.
b In a stadium during an Olympic final.
c In a desert, up a mountain, through a jungle – anywhere that nobody's been before.

What do you like most about swimming?
a Splashing around and having fun.
b Swimming lots of lengths in the pool.
c Dodging boats and sharks – it's a challenge!

What kind of holiday would you like to take?
a Staying on a campsite by a beach.
b Flying somewhere sunny where you can enjoy swimming and playing sports outdoors.
c Backpacking through a country where you've never been before and don't speak the language.

What's the best way to use a car?
a To take you where you need to go, like the shops and the cinema.
b To race around a track at top speed.
c To take part in a rally through mountains and deserts – the tougher the terrain the better.

What do you like about mountains?
a They are beautiful to look at.
b It is nice to ski and walk on mountains.
c There is nothing better than climbing a mountain to the summit and then snowboarding all the way back down.

ANSWERS:

Mostly a: You're not that bothered by adventure and like things to be comfortable and familiar. That's fine – enjoy yourself, but maybe sometimes it would be great to push yourself to try something new.

Mostly b: You're obviously very sporty and enjoy being active, but perhaps you like things to be well organized rather than too adventurous? Perhaps you could try a new activity that gets you out exploring new places sometimes.

Mostly c: You are ready to get exploring! It is great to be so adventurous, but always plan your expeditions carefully and make sure you have all the right equipment. Happy exploring!

GLOSSARY

amputate remove a body part

avalanche snowslide, where layers of snow slip down
a mountainside

carbohydrate food that gives the body energy

crevasse deep crack in ice

current movement of water in a definite direction

elite best at their sport

free climbing climbing rock faces with very little equipment

glacier huge, slowly moving block of ice

gorge deep, narrow valley

half-pipe structure used by snowboarders to perform stunts,
with sloping ramps on either side

heat exhaustion when exposure to intense heat causes
a person to feel dizzy and weak

hypothermia when exposure to cold temperatures causes
a person's body temperature to drop dangerously low

jubilant feeling of great joy, happiness, and excitement

kayak type of small canoe

kite skiing when a skier is pulled along by a kite

marathon race run over a distance of approximately
42 kilometres (a little over 26 miles)

microlight small, light aircraft that can carry only one or two people

off-piste skiing on untouched, powder snow away from the official ski runs

pacer runner who accompanies an athlete for part of a race to help him or her run a fast time

recumbent bicycle bicycle that is ridden in a lying-down position

sponsor organization or person that supports something or someone with money

stamina ability to keep going over a long period

steeplechase obstacle race in which runners have to leap over barriers

summit highest point on a mountain

tandem bicycle for two people

terrain physical features of land

tidal bore large movement of water as it pushes down a river with the changing tide

transceiver device that can send and receive communications

wetsuit suit that covers nearly the whole body to keep swimmers and divers warm

whitewater rapids fast-moving water around and over rocks with powerful currents

FIND OUT MORE

Books

10 Explorers Who Changed the World (10 Series), Clive Gifford (Kingfisher, 2008)

Hillary and Norgay's Mount Everest Adventure, Jim Kerr (Heinemann Library, 2007)

Mount Everest, Nancy Dickmann (Raintree, 2013)

The Amazon, Jane Bingham (Raintree, 2013)

Websites

www.8bridges.org
This website is full of information about the 8 Bridges Hudson River Swim and has lots of photographs of competitors.

www.alastairhumphreys.com
Find out more about Alastair Humphreys's adventures and look at his stunning photography on his own website.

www.freerideworldtour.com
Look out for news about Anne-Flore Marxer and find out about other freeriding snowboarders on this website.

www.noordinaryjoe.co.uk
Joe Simpson's website includes a gallery of photos showing some of his adventures.

www.race2recovery.com

Go to the Race2Recovery team's website to find out all about their mission to complete the Dakar Rally and their other challenges.

www.stevefisher.net

Explore Steve Fisher's website to find out more about where in the world he has explored in his kayak.

Further research

The Marathon des Sables is one of the world's most extreme ultramarathons. Find out more about other ultramarathons that take place. What makes them challenging? What sorts of people take part in these extreme running races?

Find out more about open water swimming. Do any races take place near where you live? Find out about some other great open water swimmers.

Do some research to find out about the history of the Dakar Rally. What can you discover about the routes for the race before it moved to South America?

Choose one of the adventurers mentioned in this book and find out more about his or her life and adventures. What sort of personality does he or she have? How do you think those qualities make for a good sporting adventurer?

INDEX